The Magnanimous Life of a Gifted Artist

KRYSTAL PEGRAM

ISBN: 0692746315
ISBN-13: 978-0-692-74631-8

DEDICATION

To my late grandma, Bessie Mae, for giving me your spirit.
To my late father for letting go of what you could never
keep so that I could reach the fullness of my potential.
To my amazing mom for giving me your determination
and endurance to finish what I start.
To the God of all creation, may I reflect you in all I do.

CONTENTS

ACKNOWLEDGMENTS

I am so grateful for the awesome work of Elise Macdonald for editing despite A busy schedule and for being such a great support and a great friend.

I would like to thank Marc, Kelly and Cleo for starting me on the path to write a book by drawing upon the deepest parts of me. For every "We support you" text and for literally living with me and taking care of me when I could not do so for myself, I am eternally grateful.

A special thanks to the two ministries that have loved me and supported me through the most amazing, terrifying, and challenging times of my life: Mars Hill Fellowship and Greater United in Faith. Pastors M. and J. Allwood, and J. and O. Ardayfio my appreciation for you will never reach its limits. To my Pastor-Mommy-Apostle C. Cathcart, and Co-Pastor-Aunt W. Williams and the entire Greater U family, past and present, you are the parts that make up my very soul.

To my life-group, my dope-friend, my sister-friends, my best-friendickles, my nephew, my besties, my prophet, and my family, I would have to write another book to express what you mean to me. I live my life with you and I am all the better for it.

INTRODUCTION

Why am I writing this?

I've been where you are. I've felt the same frustration. I know what it feels like to have so many things that you can do that it makes it hard to know what you should do. I know the discomfort of trying to fit all of who you are into a place that is just too small for you. I know the sting of being taken advantage of and the sadness of not being valued for who you are. I know the loneliness of being gifted beyond what you can even understand of yourself. I know how it feels to be different from the people whose circles you want to join. I know you are wondering if it is possible to make sense of the jumble of your inner creativity pointing yourself in the direction of success, peace, and happiness.

You may be asking 'How do I know if I am a gifted artist?' Before we answer this question, we should define "art". The online Oxford dictionary defines art as the expression or application of human creative skill and imagination, producing works to be appreciated primarily for their beauty or emotional power. Traditionally, art referred to painting and sculpture; however, as human thought evolved, so did our understanding of beauty. More recently, modern society has upheld other forms of expression, such as singing, dancing, writing, poetry, spoken word and poetic recitation, and acting. Furthermore each of these art forms has subsections such as comedy, fashion design, and architecture, to name a few. As we discuss gifted artists, we do so with the understanding that an artist is one who has devoted their life to the study and practice of one or more art forms.

Every artist possesses an innate ability to produce something beautiful that resonates with others in an emotional way. However, a gifted artist produces beauty that also resonates with others in a spiritual way. A gifted artist embodies not only artistic talent, but the spirit of the art form. It is the spirit of the art form that possesses the artist and leads to a lifestyle of devotion and dedication. A gifted singer or player IS Music; a gifted poet embodies the soul of rhythm and words; a gifted speaker lives within and because of the art of communication; a gifted artist lives in their art, and their art lives in them. It's in how they live, how they think, how they see the world, and how the world sees them.

A gifted artist has been created to be magnanimous. The word magnanimous is of Latin origin: The roots are magna, meaning large, and animus, meaning mind, soul or governing spirit. A gifted artist is a Great Soul. Living a magnanimous life means that every experience is great (amplified, or of heightened intensity). A gifted artist's sense of observation will be greater, with a stronger ability of discernment or empathy which serves them in knowing how their art affects (or will affect) others. They are more profoundly affected by the atmospheres surrounding them or attitudes of others, which can cause them to experience emotions more deeply than their non-artist counterparts. As you can imagine, or know firsthand, theirs is not always an easy existence. Sadly, artists too often buckle under the strain of their gifts and are crushed before they are able to celebrate the magnitude of their own greatness.

However, the hallmark of a magnanimous life is that a great soul has access to great freedom and a quality of life that is characterized by beauty, passion, and love. It is my sincere belief that, with the proper groundwork, every gifted artist can reach heights in their artistry, careers, and relationships that most others won't even dare to imagine. Therefore, I am encouraging you to lay a solid foundation so that you can build something so awesome that it will be here long after you are gone.

If you are ready to step into the artistic life that you have always felt deep inside you, this book is for you. If you are exhausted by things that do not satisfy you and long to uncover what you should be doing with your artistic life, this book is for you. If you are the parent, guardian, lover, friend, business associate, or employee of an artistic individual and you want to better understand the challenges of the gifted artist (and how you can better support their dreams and goals), this book is for you. Lastly, if you know that it's now or never to reach for your dreams, then this book is DEFINITELY for you. It is time for you to embody, without reservation, the entirety of who you are and boldly live the *Magnanimous Life of a Gifted Artist*.

WARPED PURPOSE

War-pose: A warped sense of identity upon which one sets limited goals or artistic aspirations; also called *Work-Purpose*. Setting limitations on potential pursuits based on one's perceived ability to excel or on previous success in specific endeavors that leads to the exclusion of unexplored areas of inner creativity i.e. only doing what works

HARMONIOUS IDENTITY

There are hundreds of ideas and a myriad of books written on purpose. Authors throughout the ages have discussed, at length, how to uncover, unlock, realize, and pursue purpose. Searching the web, we're overwhelmed with the number of people who are eager to give you their take on what purpose is and what you need to do to be successful and happy in the pursuit of it.

There is a prevailing sense of what I call 'War-pose': when your understanding of your life's calling is based on what you are capable of doing. For example, throughout my life, I thought I was supposed to be a gospel singer — or more specifically a Worship Leader (a church worker who engages a church congregation through numerous musical selections during a Sunday service.) The position seemed like it would be a perfect fit for me; after all, I loved music, I loved God, and I grew up in church. I was a singer, songwriter, and most importantly, I was good at it. During my first days in that role, I was floored by the fact that someone was paying me to do what I would have done (and had done previously) for free. I spent years leading with such power and enthusiasm, all the while feeling a growing sense of disconnect from what I was doing.

Then one day it finally happened: I just couldn't do it anymore. Worse yet, I couldn't understand why I didn't have any more to give. I still loved God, though I had a few issues with some of the folks he created. I still loved music, songwriting, and singing. I loved worshipping, so why was I disconnected from this particular experience? Was is just extreme tiredness? Had I lost touch with my passion or sold out to the money? After I left that position, I did not lead worship again for another three years. One night, during a time of meditation, a voice spoke within me: *"Your gifts are like an umbrella. You are a singer, performer, and worshipper. All these things are under your umbrella. When they come together, they give you the ability to perform a task and be in a certain role - but that doesn't mean that is who you are, or all that you can do. You have spent so much of your life convincing yourself that this is who you should be that you never stopped to wonder if this is who you are."*

When considering your purpose, the question you must ask yourself is "How can you live your life in harmony with your identity — rather than living a life frustrated by it?" Many gifted artists feel confused and discouraged. When one is talented in multiple areas of art it can be very difficult to know where to begin or how to make sense of a seemingly random collections of interests. The worst mistake you can make is to discard or cut away different parts of your creative anatomy in an attempt to simplify who you are, rather than seeking the path where all of your parts work together to create your artistic identity.

Questions to consider:

*Am I satisfied at the end of every day with what I have
produced?
Am I content with where I am?
Am I disconnected from what I am doing?
How often am I fully invested
emotionally/spiritually/passionately with my artistry?
Am I doing what I am doing because I was told I am good at it?*

THE MAN UPSTAIRS

Regardless of your thoughts on God and His role in humanity, you have been divinely imprinted with purpose. All of humanity was designed with purpose and on purpose. Divinity is in the DNA of a gifted artist. The nature of gifted artistry reflects The Divine in that it is inexplicable, mysterious, and marvelous to witness. To be in the presence of a gifted artist is a wonderful and awe-inspiring experience. To witness the Divine nature at work in an individual is truly mesmerizing and powerful.

Whatever you think you know of God, trust me, He's so much more than that! Typically we understand God based on experiences and a limited affiliation with Him. Too often He is viewed as "the man upstairs". Many religions highlight specific attributes of God that are humanistic; while these attributes frame Him in such a way that He is more relatable, it is extremely important to understand that humanity has been given His qualities — not the other way around. God is not an invention of creation; rather, creation is an extension of God. We do ourselves a disservice when we examine God through the lens of our own limitations. He is without limits. He is vast and inexhaustible. No matter how much we search Him, we cannot — and will never — find His limits.

This is why God is bigger than religion. I'm not saying this to incite heresy. Nor am I saying this in an attempt to be anti-religion. I am, however, challenging you to detach your view of God from the limits of religion. Religion is a construct. Sometimes helpful, sometimes detrimental, but always limited. If we rely on religion to comprehensively inform us of the character and nature of God, we will be misinformed, ignorant, and deceived. Religion is in many ways a snapshot of God. No matter how high the definition is on a picture, it can never compare to the experience of being around the subject of the photo. The universe reflects the size of God while eternity denotes His lifespan. God is vast and infinite.

Because of the divine source from which gifted artistry originates it, too, is limitless. The limitations of the gifts exist in the mind of the artist. When a gifted artist finds the strength to shed the mental barriers that exist between what they think they can accomplish and what they actually can accomplish, they access their own divinity. For a gifted artist to live without mental limits is for that artist to unlock the same creativity and ingenuity that was present at the dawn of the universe.

The walls that create mental barriers are composed of different materials. For some, mental limits are made of negative words or forces that discourage the full operation of higher and deeper levels of creativity. Sometimes this negativity stands alone, while at other times it attaches to insecurities and fears that already existed in a person's heart or mind. Therefore, before you can fully live a magnanimous life, you must level the walls that stop you from accepting who you are.

Questions to consider:

What do I believe regarding God and my own divine nature?
How has religion shaped my view of God?
What can be categorized as divine nature or God being present in my artistry?
What mental limitations have I set that prevent or prohibit me from seeing the vast nature of God in myself?

THE TRIFECTA OF TERROR

I refer to Doubt, Fear, and Insecurity as the trifecta of terror. These three destructive forces relentlessly battle with the minds of gifted individuals and are the enemies of your soul. They are not the result of human creation; they are not extensions of our emotions. They are adversarial, dark forces whose sole mission is to delay, stop, or abort the purpose assigned to you. When you surrender your mind to them, you disconnect yourself from the power and authority of your creativity.

DOUBT

Doubt is not just disbelief; it is the inability to believe. Doubt always resonates with me very personally because I have faced it in myself far more than I care to admit. It is the most cancerous of the trifecta, because it tends to spread — poisoning your thoughts, feelings, and clouding your emotions and judgment.

A doubt-filled argument is one based on inability. Doubt is a coward that has the audacity to accuse you of being incapable of doing that which you were by nature created to do. If you have been created to do something, why would you be unable to do it? That would be the same as a tree saying to itself "*I don't think I am able to do this tree thing*". It seems ridiculous, but it happens constantly in the minds of gifted artists.

Let's discuss doubt and desire. Typically, when we have doubts, they are in direct opposition to our heart's desire. For a moment, let's move away from thinking in artistic terms. Let's think of a basic desire for most, if not all of humanity: the desire for love. Doubt will say "*you will never know what true love is*," or "*you will never be successful in a relationship*," or "*no one will ever love you*." These are all false statements. The reason they are false is because you possess the desire for such things. It is impossible for us to desire what does not exist — or to desire something that will not manifest itself at some point in our lives. If you possess the desire for something, that is because the thing you desire exists in this world. That internal desire is both a magnet and a compass. You possess one half; its polar opposite exists someplace else. Desire causes you to be drawn to the object of your desire.

Pure desire is different from corrupted desire, which causes covetousness, greed, and jealousy. Pure desire does not seek to gain what does not belong to itself; rather, it will bring you to your divine destiny. Whatever has led you to this precise moment in your life has been designed and orchestrated to strengthen your resolve and purify your desire. Each challenge that you face is created to cause you to grow in a specific way. You must take the daunting steps that lead to exploration, discovery, growth and success. If you are to reach your divine destiny, you must allow the doubts that you are holding to be expressed and dispelled: it is OK for you to admit your doubts, as long as you do so with the understanding that you will accomplish what you have been created to achieve.

At the heart of a gifted artist is pure desire. Pure desire is so much more than just wanting a person or a place; it is a longing for a specific state of being. The desire to be in love is more than just wanting to possess the heart of another; rather, it's the need to exist in a perpetual state of intimacy. It is the same with gifted artistry: when you distill the truth at the heart of your artistic desire, you will find that your desire is far more noble than you may have originally thought. Therein lies the magnanimous nature of desire.

FEAR

Fear is a paralyzing dark force. Fear is so worshipped that it has become a god to many individuals without their knowledge. Many people worship at the altar of fear; they offer their hopes, dreams, relationships, and aspirations to it. Fear is the voice that whispers in secret. In the gifted individual, Fear can produce powerful images and thoughts that will appear to be just as authentic as those that come from the gifts. Often thoughts and dreams that are produced from Fear will resonate with the dreamer or the thinker in a nagging and haunting manner. Fear will constantly tell you what you cannot have and try to convince you of what you cannot achieve. Fear will cause your very own mind or heart to betray you. For many gifted artists, the fear of exposure locks them in chains and stops them from sharing their craft without reservation.

Stage fright is a type of fear. It is a performance anxiety that can cause physical distress to the body, resulting in sweating, an inability to speak or move, nausea, and even fainting. For many artists, the thought of being onstage or in a public space is terrifying because of extreme exposure. The feeling that we call "stage fright" is nearly the equivalent of what a rape victim may experience: the feeling of violation without recourse or protection. I must admit that as a child I experienced stage fright: I was often asked to sing in churches, but was terrified because I was bullied at school so mercilessly that I expected to be ridiculed. My mother would have to take me into the bathroom and give me and encouraging talk for at least 30 minutes before I shakily would step on stage to sing. I now know what she was doing was combating and confronting fear. Far too often, gifted artists give in to fear and don't fight it.

The first step towards combating fear is finding the courage of Love. The greatest force stronger than Fear is Love. In order to boldly display your artistry you must love both your gifts and yourself. Stage fright comes from the fear of being rejected. When we love ourselves and appreciate our gifts, we will be more willing to share them. When my mother spoke to me in those moments of stage fright, she said that God had placed in me was put there for others. She would say to me "sing under the anointing". In the Christian faith, the anointing is a supernatural endowment of power that rests upon individuals in a unique manner. So when she told me to use my "anointing," she was encouraging me to access a divine strength and courage to operate freely in my own artistic greatness, which allowed me to understand that when I sang or performed I was doing so with strength and empowerment that came from an external source. Friend, this is what I am sharing with you. The fact that you are gifted means you have also been endowed with a power to express your artistry to the world without the fear of the world rejecting what you have to give. The truth is that the world needs you to be confident and bold.

Now I understand that this sentiment might make you feel all warm and fuzzy, but the challenging part of conquering fear is the action that you must take; it is very easy to feel confident from your seat. Ultimately, you are going to have to do it!

I believe very strongly in exposure therapy; I have witnessed the powerful effect of it in my own life. I must be honest here. Even after those long pep talks with my mom, I still was nervous when I stepped on stage, but my mother would not allow me to "chicken out". The bottom line is, You HAVE to get over your fears by doing the very thing that makes you afraid. For performers this means that you must perform. When you find the courage to expose yourself, it will be easier to share the next time. I honestly can say, I rarely get nervous when it comes time for me to sing. I have developed more than a sense of confidence in my own abilities; I understand the responsibility I have to those around me. That is not to say that I don't feel fearful when facing new challenges, but I know within my soul that my artistry cannot coexist with fear.

INSECURITY

The third of the menacing three is Insecurity: a dark force that leads one to abort purpose. Insecurity is called by many different names including low self-esteem and self-doubt. Insecurity is the awkward younger sibling of Pride. Pride and Insecurity are related because they both warp how you view yourself. Pride convinces you of your own importance while Insecurity convinces you of your unimportance. They both demand you prove yourself and neither will ever be satisfied with you no matter what you do. They are selfish in nature and will divert all of your energy and attention inward rather than on positively affecting the lives of others. Insecurity is fed by comparison; the more you compare who you are and the gifts you have to someone else, the greater Insecurity will grow in you.

There are many reasons artists compare themselves to each other. However, the most fundamental reason is the innate instinct of our animalistic nature. At the time of our conception we were formed by the fastest, strongest sperm breaking through the egg. After birth the majority of what was learned was to ensure personal survival and the survival of the human species. A survivalist's mentality suggests that only the strong survive. It is no wonder that most bring that survivalist instinct into their artistry. Many gifted artists have not shed the sense of "survival of the fittest" and therefore treat artistry as an eat-or-be-eaten blood sport. When artists live by comparison, they fail to embrace the nurture instinct of our species.

Nurture helps us tap into a fundamental truth; we are stronger together than we are apart. Gifted artistry is fortified when we embrace the strength inherent in being together. This understanding challenges us to embrace what we can bring to a group or artistic community. It helps us to properly assess the strengths and value of others and ourselves. There is no better way to shed your insecurities than to surround yourself with people who will encourage, uplift, and foster the growth and use of your gifted artistry.

Questions to Consider:

What are my heart's desires for my art?
What corruptions have I allowed to infiltrate these desires?
How can I safeguard against corrupted desires?
How far am I willing to go and how much am I willing to sacrifice for the sake of my desires?
What are some of the ways I succumb to fear?
How can I challenge myself to overcome or face my fear(s)?
What is one step I can do today to overcome my fear and express my creativity?
How have I compared myself to other artists?
What are some characteristics I value in the artists that I have compared myself to?
How can I create or join an artistic community?
What can I offer an artistic community?
What can I gain from an artistic community?
What can I do today to foster a healthier artistic community?

THE UMBRELLA

The Umbrella, or Parasol, dates back to ancient civilizations spanning thousands of years into the past. It has evolved alongside humanity covering many heads, from ancient kings to peasants. Initially regarded as a luxury of palace royalty, the humble umbrella nearly vanished from use. It was restored to prominence by French nobility during the Renaissance Era. This resilient piece of technology has remained virtually unaltered in its design and has evolved in its usage from providing shade from the sun, to protection from the rain, to weathering the most brutal of wind storms. The following sections will explore the noble umbrella and how it metaphorically personifies the design and make-up of a gifted artist.

THE PEAK: SEX AND THE SPIRIT

The Peak (or the Ferrule) of an Umbrella is the topmost point, which binds all the components of the umbrella together. The peak is one of the smaller pieces of the anatomy of an Umbrella, and yet it's such a vital part of its function and mechanics. The Peak of yourself is the same; it encompasses the totality of who you are. The Peak harkens back to our previous discussion of divinely imprinted identity, and is the area of concentrated purpose and identity. You will find that through the course of your life you will come to understand your Peak in greater detail and with increased clarity. The Peak lives and breathes in everything you do and is composed of two equally important elements: Spirituality and Sexuality. If you can uncover and fully grasp each element, you will be able to fundamentally define who you are.

Spirituality and Sexuality are our two supreme governing bodies; unfortunately, they are often pitted against each other. If you are more aligned or in tune with one, then you typically will have less understanding or development of the other. The developed gifted person is one who lives a life with their sexual and spiritual identity in healthy balance. Sexuality and Spirituality are fundamentally the same, yet serve two different functions. Spirituality functions to connect us with God and the divine, while Sexuality connects us with Humanity. Spirituality and Sexuality are reflections of each other. The needs of humanity mandate what transpires in the spirit world — and the will and purpose of God is reflected in sexual desires. This means that who you are spiritually will be reflected in your sexuality, and vice versa.

SEXUALITY

Sexuality is a beautiful part of humanity; it possess the divine nature of its creator. It bears His signature and He delights very much in its expression. It is His gift to humanity. It was created as a means of sustenance and repopulation; He made it enjoyable to ensure that we would continually engage in it. God LOVES sex. There are some who would lead you to believe that the problems that exist in the world boil down to too much sex. Don't get me wrong: we are bombarded with sexual images and suggestive media on a daily basis. However, these images are meant to distract us from our sexual identity, not celebrate it; we should take issue with that. According to the laws of supply and demand, if the market place is oversaturated by a product, the product's value declines. In essence, sex has been devalued because there's too much of it available. While this situation is problematic and we must work to create a healthier sexual cultural dynamic, we must resist the urge to swing the pendulum in the opposite direction towards suppression.

Our sexual nature should never be suppressed. To suppress one's sexuality is to ignore or resist the fulfillment of innate sexual needs and desires in an attempt to forcibly control or eliminate it. When sexuality is suppressed, it will express itself in deviant behavior. Sexual attraction and desire cause a natural buildup of pressure which must be released. If you have not created healthy ways to express your sexual self, you will experience the breaking of the proverbial dam. Sexual suppression not only causes uncontrollable deviant behavior; it also discourages and impairs healthy artistic and gifted creativity. Your sexuality is such a large part of your human identity that if you constantly suppress it or refuse to acknowledge it, you are cutting yourself off from yourself, which can lead to confusion and frustration.

The challenge for many gifted individuals is to avoid corrupting or otherwise defiling their inner being in the process of uncovering sexual identity. For gifted individuals, empowerment lives in being the owner of your sexual identity, not the victim of it. If you have fear in the area of your sexuality, you have failed to embody who you are. It is only when you walk in the fullness of your sexual and spiritual self that your artistic gifts are able to operate at a peak capacity.

SPIRITUALITY

Spirituality refers to what animates and makes us conscious living beings. Spirituality challenges prevailing knowledge, cultural mores, religious doctrine, and scientific theories and will often defy logic. The spiritual world that gifted individuals are connected to is vast and infinite. A developed gifted individual will live with a heightened level of spiritual sensitivity. The gifted are, or should be, in tune with the intangible things that are a part of the invisible spiritual world. When you develop your ability to tune into what resonates in your spirit, you will increase your ability to hear the voice of God in a through your art.

Spirituality is more than a gut feeling. It is the resonation of a greater, deeper truth that echoes in your inner being. Your spiritual self is the living vibrant reflection of God and constantly seeks to be connected to Him. This connection is what gives access to the world of the spirit. It is through this connection that we have divine empowerment to fulfill the purpose of our craft. Your areas of authority and your convictions combined with your passions make up your Spiritual identity.

The best way to heighten and increase the awareness of your spiritual identity is through inner reflection; you must take time to still yourself and silence the voices that compete for your attention. You may find a great need to unplug from various forms of media: digital, print, and social. In so doing, you'll empty the storehouses of your spirit of everyday noise. Afterwards, I encourage you to sit in the silence and the stillness of being empty. Take note of two important things: what comes from you and what fills you. Our entire spiritual identity can be distilled to what goes into our spirit and what comes from it.

What are your spiritual markers? Are there certain attributes or patterns that you can note? Are you altruistic, empathetic, strong, sensitive, nurturing, protective, etc. What draws people to you? When answering these questions, also note what things affect your spirit — what things surround you that have a positive or negative affect on your spiritual temperature. Note what makes you feel sad, angry, uplifted, discouraged, happy, joyful, depressed, understood, loved, etc.: these factors comprise the details of your spiritual identity.

Questions to Consider:

How can you explore and express your sexuality in a spiritually safe and personally healthy way?
On a scale of 1-10 (10 being the greatest), how well are you in touch with your sexuality? Spirituality?
What are your preferred sexual and spiritual expressions?
What sexual and spiritual outlets do you have in place?
How effective are they in releasing building sexual pressure and expressing your spiritual self?

METAL CONNECTORS:
CREATIVE THEOLOGY

In an umbrella, the Metal Connectors are pieces that attach the cloth covering on the outside of the umbrella to the other mechanical hardware on the inside of the umbrella. They are reinforcement parts that help the umbrella to have and hold its shape when opened and expanded. Similarly, an artist's belief system or Creative Theology gives shape to his or her artistry.

Creative Theology is the rationale, system of beliefs, and integrity of what you do. A gifted artist must have a clearly defined Creative Theology. Simply put, you have to believe in something. You must have so much allegiance to that belief that you are willing to devote your life to it, be willing to suffer for it, and (if necessary) die for it. This theology will be the bedrock of your artistry and will help to keep you grounded and centered. It will decrease your susceptibility to being swayed or losing yourself to the temptation and allure of artistic corruption. As you begin to build and frame your Creative Theology, you should consider your Artistic Needs.

An Artistic Need can be defined as something that is

essential to the creative function of an individual. There are two types of needs: outflowing and inflowing. Both outflowing and inflowing needs are places that are vulnerable to corruption. Therefore every artist must identify their needs and how they can satisfy these needs on a consistent basis. When we have a need that is unmet, it can cause a sense of desperation. When a gifted artist becomes desperate to fulfill a need, he or she is more willing to compromise in their Creative Theology.

An outflowing need is what a gifted artist must produce or share with the whomever or whatever surrounds them (this is not the same as a pressure outlet, which we will discuss later.) An outflowing need is an internal mandate to express one's artistry and creativity. Take, for example, the Communicator. This artist will constantly feel the need to talk, or share thoughts, feelings, or information. This outflowing need, if left unmet, can become a compulsion: a need that cannot be managed or bridled, which happens when gifted artists fail to acknowledge and express outflowing needs. One of the healthiest ways to meet an outflowing artistic need is practice. If you are a gifted artist, you MUST develop a consistent practice schedule. Practice will allow you to develop different expressions of your creativity and provide a consistent outlet for your outflowing need.

An inflowing need is something that must be received to sustain the production of creativity. To determine the nature of an inflowing artistic need, ask yourself: *"Can I create without this? If I create without this, will it affect what I produce, the way or method in which I produce, or the quality of what I produce?"* Above all, you must determine if the inflowing need is detrimental to your physical, spiritual, emotional, or creative well being.

While inflowing needs differ greatly amongst gifted artists, one need that is universal is the need for praise. Praise is a form of encouragement that drives and fuels a gifted artist. Praise, for the gifted artist, ignites a passion and desire to be better and produce more. When a gifted artist is in a praise-less environment, he or she will find it easy to produce less or produce work of lesser quality. This need is why audience applause accompanies most performing artistic presentations.

Managing the inflowing need for praise can be challenging; artists should not live an artistic life constantly begging to be praised or applauded. This compulsion can cause performance anxiety and can disrupt creative flow. I advise artists to never ask for applause, but rather just to be applause-worthy. When you are fully invested mentally, spiritually, and emotionally in what you are producing, praise will find its way to you. Conversely, if you are performing or presenting your art, it is fine to express appreciation for the generosity of a certain response. For example, before performing a song, an artist can encourage the audience to sing along, clap, or "make some noise" if audience members feel moved to do so. There is nothing wrong with gently encouraging, but be careful in your approach, as you can offend your audience if you make applauding mandatory. Think of applauding like a tip for wait staff: it should be appreciated, not expected, and the recipient should be gracious and grateful, no matter how much or how little is given. Above all, you must understand that applause should be at the discretion of your fans or supporters.

Questions to Consider:

What word or phrase describes my artistic ideology?
What are my artistic needs? Inflowing/Outflowing?
How am I currently managing my needs?
How can I create a space that fosters my creativity?
How can I make this space mobile?
How can I safeguard myself from developing a praise addiction?

RIBS: CREATIVE EXPRESSION

The ribs, or metal struts, of an umbrella form quadrants or sections. Each quadrant is formed when two ribs meet at the peak, or ferrule, and run down to the bottom of the cloth covering. When an umbrella is in use, the engagement of the metal connectors expands, pushing these ribs out and away from each other. Much like the multiple ribs of an umbrella, gifted artists tend to have interests in multiple forms of artistic expression. They may not overlap and may vary greatly from each other. I believe a gifted artist is one who embraces all the sections of their artistry, allowing for a greater flow of creativity.

For example, one of my clients, a professional musician and singer, shared during one of our development sessions that when she hears music, she visualizes colors and images. As an exercise, I encouraged her to sketch and paint what she saw while music played. What resulted was remarkable. By allowing these two ribs to connect (painting and music), she discovered a new section of her artistry that she'd previously considered to be two distinct, separate, and unrelated areas. Additionally she found that her painting was enhanced by combining another form of artistic expression.

The great challenge for many artists is making sense of unrelated interests — a particularly challenging task when an artist is unsure of who he or she is holistically. Confusion of artistic purpose typically happens because most artists believe that they should only focus on one expression, which can lead to creative frustration. This thinking is not only warped, but also creatively discouraging and dangerous. If you find that you enjoy singing or dancing just as much as you enjoy acting or painting, then you should understand that all of these things are expressions of your whole artistic self. Just because you may be "better" or more exercised in one expression, you must not conflate that fact with thinking that the preferred form of expression must be the only expression. To be a well-balanced gifted artist, you must endeavor to make room for all of your creative expressions and place equal importance on them, regardless of your perceived level of technical attainment in those areas. Other artistic expressions are important parts of your artistic make-up, ultimately making you a stronger umbrella and a stronger artist.

Questions to Consider:

What is my preferred expression of artistry?
What fragments of artistic expression seem to not fit with anything else?
How can I incorporate or explore other artistic forms?
What interest or hobby have I deemed less important in order to focus on my preferred expression?
What unique work/artistic structure would allow me to exercise all of my creative self?

COVERING: BRAND AND IMAGE

Umbrellas come in various colors and textures of coverings. The cloth covering of an umbrella reflects the way image and branding operate in a gifted artist. As a gifted artist, your image and your brand are important, as they both function through what you present to your fans, consumers, supporters, and creative peers. The difference between image and branding is that an artist's brand is a picture that represents what they produce, while their image is a picture of who they are.

An artist's image and brand should be crafted so that they reflect a well-considered, intentional snapshot of who the artist is and the focus areas of the artistry. A solid image and brand is a translation of the inner creativity of an artist, not a contrived persona (or fictional character.) Portraying a character may be acceptable for a while, but imagine having to wake up every day and pretend to be someone else. It will become exhausting and burdensome, fading over time. When your image reflects your creative theology, it will be well received by your audience without being a burden to your artistry.

The most sustainable image is one that is based on the truth of who you are. If your image is based on who you want to be rather than who you are, you may slowly be crushed by an image that is bigger and heavier than yourself. Conversely, don't shortchange your supporters or yourself by having an image that is one-dimensional or not engaging. A one-dimensional image is a surface approach in which an artist only considers the visual aspects of their image. It is true that you should consider appearance details such as your wardrobe, physique, clothing style, color scheme etc.; however, non-visual aspects of your image are equally important. For example, if your image is "mysterious and alluring," then every time you interact with anyone, you should embody mystery and allure. It should be seen not only in the way you dress, but also the way you behave, the way you speak, and your mannerisms. Your energy and presence should exude mystery and allure.

When taking my clients through the process of image consulting, I encourage them to dissect the more unique parts of their personalities. Examine your quirks or oddities; it's beneficial to study the parts of you that are uncommon or nonsensical. A well-balanced image is both unique and relatable. As you craft your image, look at everything about yourself; exclude nothing and remember to be exacting and meticulous. Be sure to not leave out factors that you consider to be flaws: many successful actors, comedians, singers, poets, activists, and painters have had identifying marks or features that became iconic. You may have a feature that you dislike or hate that could be the very thing that makes you noticeable. A gifted artist appreciates everything about themselves, even their flaws.

A well chosen image is balanced by a strong brand. The strongest of brands are lifestyle brands, which focus on artistry that produces something that people will integrate as vital or significant to their lives. A lifestyle brand is one that consumers are loyal to, to the extent that the brand becomes synonymous with an activity, hobby, or routine apart of "everyday life". The more embedded the routine, the more loyal a person will be to the brand. As a gifted artist, your brand should answer a fundamental question or problem; people will look to you to provide something that is of value to their lives. So when defining your brand, ask yourself how what you're offering is needed or important to others.

When crafting your image and brand, be sure to consider how they will be reflected online, specifically in social media environments. A social media platform can be a merciless, unflinching microscope that can either destroy you or empower you as an artist. While you cannot control what people will say or do online, you can mentally insulate yourself. A good image can provide a protective layer between you and social commentators; a strong brand can help you to create a positive social environment for your artistry.

A GIFTED ARTISTS' GUIDE TO THE INTERNET:

The following is a list of things to keep in mind when you are establishing your online presence.

A. You are a Business; ultimately, you are providing a good and/or service. Everything you do in public will affect your business, so make sure you are doing what is in its best interest, including what you wear, whom you endorse or associate with, and where you go. Remember what happens on the internet STAYS on the internet ... forever.

B. You don't need EVERYONE to like you. Brand and image are derived from business models used by all successful companies; just like those companies, you must understand that your artistry may not be attractive to certain segments of the population, no matter how developed your artistry is. Keep in mind people have varied tastes and palettes; do not be offended if a person or group of people do not like what you do. You are not devalued by others' tastes in the slightest; rather you should be encouraged to produce for the people who need and appreciate who you are.

C. Don't always ignore the Critics. Criticism can elevate your artistry by causing you to analyze what you do, spurring you to dig deeper. Criticism can help you assess whether the masses are able to grasp your artistic concept or creative vision. As a gifted artist, it will be up to you to decide how much criticism you can safely subject yourself to without becoming discouraged. Criticism has its place in artistry; it will be your job to keep a healthy balance between truth and honesty versus praise and support.

D. Don't feed the Trolls. Troll: a person who makes comments to incite arguments or gain attention by being negative or offensive. The security of anonymity means that trolls can say cruel things that they would never dare say to another human face to face. Nothing can destroy a good Image and Brand quicker than engaging with a negative commentator online. Honestly, you have better things to do with your time and energy.

Questions to Consider:

What truthful things do I want people to see or think about me?
What are my most noticeable attributes or features?
How can I embrace the features that I don't like?
How can those become iconic symbols of my brand and image?
Thinking about my primary artistic expressions, what qualities set me apart from others?
Whom do I trust to offer me constructive criticism?
What societal and cultural problem(s) bother me the most?
What problem(s) do I think my artistry can solve?
How does my brand address a fundamental human need?
Do I have a healthy balance of social media and real-world interaction?

WIND VENTS: WORK TO FAIL; PLAY TO WORK

The wind vents on an umbrella are slits that allow air to pass through the covering: a built-in pressure release system. Umbrellas without this feature are more prone to flip inside out in heavy winds. Once an umbrella flips inside out, its integrity is compromised because the metal connectors have been stretched and bent out of shape. You must be sure to protect the integrity of your artistic umbrella by recognizing your need for continual pressure release. But first, let's discuss a healthy work schedule.

As a gifted artist, you should take on the mindset of working to fail, an idea which comes from health/physical education. When lifting weights to increase strength, the goal is to do as many repetitions as possible, until your muscles can no longer engage, or working the muscle until it fails. As a gifted artist, your daily goal in terms of creatively engaging yourself should be the same. In doing so, you are flexing your creative muscles and strengthening your artistic self. A great way to ensure a productive work day is to create a schedule before you start creating: map out times when you will take a break, eat, and when you will stop working for the day. By breaking up your day, you will create peak production hours while also promoting physical and mental health. The goal is to build a structured schedule around your natural creative rhythm. After creating a schedule, honor it by not running late or deviating from it. When you respect your schedule, you create a healthy creative work life with proper respect given to work and rest.

While there are times when you must put in long hours and devote a great deal of energy to a task or project, it is important to not overwork yourself. Overworking yourself is when you engage yourself creatively, mentally or physically to the point of exhaustion, which can and will lead to burn-out. When a gifted artist burns out it can take months or years to feel inspired to create again. The goal is to live a magnanimous life of balance and artistic longevity, which means allowing time for proper rest, powering down completely, and allowing your mind and your spirit to decompress. Rest will help you to feel rejuvenated when you begin a new work day. The other component to a magnanimous creative work-life and your artistic health is having time to play.

I know many artists who will spend all day practicing or creating, but fail to take time to have social interactions. As a human being your have an inherent need to interact with others; therefore, you should not approach your artistic life with different expectations. Don't disconnect yourself from others in the pursuit of your artistic success; be sure to balance your week with social engagements and significant interactions to help clear your mind. Be sure to refocus your energy as well. It's fine to discuss your projects with friends and loved ones, but you will defeat the purpose of spending time with them if you are mentally preoccupied with the tasks you are working on.

Another element of taking time for play is rewarding yourself; I encourage you to enjoy the fruits of your labors. You can do so by celebrating the completion of every project. Also, when you are paid, set aside a certain amount of money that is strictly for entertainment and recreation.

In finding ways to celebrate and relieve stress, I caution you to beware of excess when it comes to alcohol consumption or drug use: keep in mind that they can impair your creative flow and, if enjoyed to excess, can cause delays and your having to devote time to recovery. As a gifted artist, you are responsible for knowing your limits and tolerance levels. Surround yourself with those who will celebrate responsibly while looking out for your wellbeing. Most importantly, if you struggle with overindulging, there is no shame in asking for help.

Questions to Consider:

How am I currently managing stress?
What is my creative work schedule?
How much time can I spend creating before I need a break?
What are my most effective ways of releasing pressure?
How do I have fun?
How do I/will I celebrate my accomplishments?
What percentage of my income will go to play?
How do I currently abuse substances or unhealthily engage in activities?
Do I feel I need assistance in practicing restrain with some vices?

THE "ME" IN TEAM

To have a magnanimous life as a gifted artist you must give care to the areas of your life that directly affect your artistry: your relationships and jobs. The more care you take when developing personal and business relationships, as well as taking jobs that serve your purpose, the stronger your artistic foundation will be.

The magnanimous life of a gifted artist is full of healthy personal relationships. Therefore you must approach making friends in a different manner than building your fan base. When building relationships, focus on quality, not simply on quantity. I wholeheartedly oppose the idea of befriending people because of what they can do for you. While I can see the value of having access to people who can get you into certain places or do specific things for you, these relationships tend to be superficial and short-lived. When meeting a new potential friend, consider what value you can add to their life before thinking of what they can add to yours. You may find that the only benefits you can provide for each other are goods or services. If that is the case, then you may choose to continue with the relationship. However, do so with the knowledge that it is transactional in nature and it may not lead to a personal connection. Transactional relationships can end once a service has been provided or a good has been delivered. To avoid misunderstandings or misleading expectations, be honest with yourself about the nature of any relationship, and be upfront with the person about how close you want to feel to them.

As a gifted artist, it is very easy for people to feel connected to you while you feel little to no connection to them, because your life is on display and your soul is laid bare. Your fans and supporters may feel that your artistry speaks directly to their life or reflects their heart. These feelings and can create a sense of bonding to you that will most often be one-sided. Therefore, you must take care to not raise the expectations of people who want to be closer to you than you feel comfortable with. You must also be careful not to take advantage of the generosity of overzealous fans; it may seem unfair that this task falls to you, but being gifted is a privilege and a responsibility. While it will benefit the business aspect of your artistry to have transactional types of relationships, it will be healthier if your personal relationships are based on deeper intangible needs such as trust, support, love, encouragement, loyalty, respect, and honesty.

When developing relationships there are a few key principles to keep in mind.

1. **Be honest.** Endeavor to tell the truth as much as possible. Don't just tell the whole truth; tell the hard truth. You may find it particularly difficult to be honest about the things you need from others. However, it will benefit your overall health if you can find the courage to do so. Relationships work best when each person is truthful about what they need and can give.

2. **Be direct.** Clearly, concisely tell others what you

need or want. Being direct means that you do not waiver in what you want, or settle for something that comes close but doesn't reach the mark. It is particularly important to be direct in business relationships. If you don't seem confident with what you need, people will give you what they feel is best for you, which can lead to unstable relationships due to insecurity and dissatisfaction.

3. **Be loyal.** Loyalty seems like a lost art-form. Trust me, it still goes a long way. I encourage you to choose wisely when you give your loyalty, but solid friends are worth it. Being loyal means you have committed to a relationship in your heart as well as with your actions, and are willing to put in the effort it takes to support the relationship. It means you are willing to defend and support your friend and expect the same in return.

4. **Be selective.** Not everyone can be a friend to you even if you are a friend to them. It may be difficult, but cut away dead weight. If are in a one-sided relationship where you are investing but the other person is not reciprocating, and you have addressed the issues with this person to no avail, it may be time to move on. Your gifted artistry is precious; you must carefully select those who will have access to your inner-workings.

Lastly, the most important relationship that you must keep in constant health is the one you have with yourself. Your personal demons can and will manifest themselves. It is your responsibility to yourself to deal with your own issues. You cannot solve other peoples' problems or be beneficial or helpful to anyone when you are not able to help yourself. Seek counseling if you feel that some issues are too overwhelming to work through alone. Remember, everyone has issues — so there is no need to feel embarrassed or ashamed of yours.

BUILDING A STRONG TEAM

As a gifted artist you must understand that you need a team working alongside you who supports the vision and mission of your artistry. Building a strong team is like the foundation of a house: the more solid it is, the longer it will support the structure on top of it. You may find that in the beginning stages of your artistic career, you'll collaborate with other artists. When collaborating with others or creating a team, be sure to honor your creative theology and assess that of those with whom you work. No two artists are the same; therefore, their versions of creative theology may differ. These differences do not mean that you should not work with artists who do not share your ideology, but be aware that those differences may affect your creative synergy and your artistic relationship.

Questions to answer when building a team:

1. What type of team do I need?
2. What are specific job functions and duties for each role?
3. When and how do I plan to compensate these people?
4. If employing family or friends, how will I candidly address issues, should the need arise?
5. Who do I or will I trust with my money?
6. Who will I trust to make decisions in my absence or if I am unable to make them for myself?
7. How will I ensure the safety and emotional well being of significant other and/or children in the selection of the members of my team?
8. How will I assess the team's progress? How will I

conduct performance reviews?

JOBS AND GIGS

When selecting jobs or taking gigs, be sure to look at the overall benefit of the task and not just the financial benefit. The goal of a gifted artist should be to do things that will foster creativity or build artistic character. To avoid frustration and live a magnanimous life, always consider how you will benefit in the long-run. If you find that a job may be financially beneficial but may not provide any creative or artistic growth, it may be better overall to turn it down.

The same applies to taking gigs or performances. I am not encouraging you to not perform in certain places because the venue might be humble or small and may provide less exposure; I have performed in many smaller spaces and grown tremendously from doing so. Rather, I am suggesting that in everything you agree to do, consider the impact it will have on you as an artist and as a person. If you find that you have done a certain type of gig repeatedly and are no longer growing from the experience, it is likely time to stretch yourself and do something different.

Questions to Consider:

How much time and energy do I dedicate to fostering healthy relationships with the people that I already know?
Do I have space in my life for new relationships?
When meeting new fans and supporters how will I ensure I am not setting unrealistic expectations or giving misleading impressions?
How would I ideally like to take advantage of my status, fame, or success?
How do I select my engagements (gigs)?
How do I assess the productivity and success of my gigs?
How will each new gig support my career aspirations?

Finally, my friend, remember this is your magnanimous life journey. Never allow the fear of change or the unknown to deter you from believing in your dreams and setting out to realize them. You will come to a place when it's time to bet on yourself. So summon up the strength and mental fortitude to do so. Never forget: a leap of faith starts with a step of courage.

ABOUT THE AUTHOR

Krystal "Krys P" Pegram is the founder and CEO of Well Done ProduKtions, an arts and entertainment company. She founded Well Done ProduKtions in 2015 upon the mission to be a global leader in artist development focusing on foundational principles that lead to artistic longevity and success. Currently Well Done ProduKtions serves artists who focus on music performance, fashion design, and literary art with projections to include artists in the areas of theatre and film & television as well.

Krystal is a singer-songwriter with multiple degrees including a B.A. in Theatre with a concentration in directing. She is an alumni of the University of North Carolina and Berklee College of Music. Her wealth of professional and artistic expertise spans from the financial world to the entertainment business. She is a celebrated artistic leader having received the Berklee Urban Service Award for her work as a community arts advocate in 2015.

She can be characterized as a counselor, a teacher, a woman of great passion and zeal, a protector and warrior in spirit. It is with great passion and strong conviction she is leading generations to discover, uncover, and serve their life's purpose with magnitude and majesty.